About Mother Geneviève G.

Marcelle Gallois (1888-1962) was the daughter of an anticlerical civil servant and spent her early life studying art in Paris. In 1917, she experienced a spiritual crisis that prompted her to enter the Benedictine convent in the rue Monsieur in Paris. However, her intense personality and temperament were such that she struggled in the religious life. Her eagerness to embrace the austerity of convent life adversely affected her health, and her art possessed a character of modernity that the nuns found strange and disturbing. She finally professed her final vows in 1939, at the age of 51. It was after this period that her work in line drawing, painting and stained glass gained recognition and acclaim outside the convent, having been noticed by an art collector who saw her work at a church sale. Since the late 1950s, her work has been displayed in several museums and is considered among the more beautiful modern depictions of monastic life.

About *The Life of Little Saint Placid*:

(from the original jacket flap:)

The extraordinary thing about Mother Gallois's book is its vigor and originality. There is no "prettiness" in her art. It is direct, astringent, powerful. As she tells the life of St. Placid, from his entry into the monastery to his death—a life devoted to prayer and contemplation, to service and love—it appears as a great spiritual adventure, an adventure in which all who have chosen the religious life are engaged.

Mother Gallois's book is contemporary in the best sense: it speaks to men and women of today, with intelligence, with humor, and with a rare theological discernment. In the development of this little monk's obscure and hidden existence there is a dynamism and strength that carries the reader along until, like St. Placid, "he is swept away by the tremendous torrent of Divine Life."

THE LIFE OF
Little Saint Placid

by

MOTHER GENEVIÈVE GALLOIS
O.S.B.

Foreword by

Marcelle Auclair

2017

ST. AUGUSTINE ACADEMY PRESS
HOMER GLEN, ILLINOIS

This book was originally published in France
©1953 by Desclée de Brouwer.

This reprint is based on the English edition
©1956 by Pantheon Books.

Reprinted with permission in 2017
by St. Augustine Academy Press

ISBN: 978-1-936639-84-7

Translated by the Monks of Mount Saviour Monastery.

To learn more about Mother Geneviève's art, visit:
https://amisggallois.wixsite.com/ggallois

FOREWORD

IN A CERTAIN BENEDICTINE CONVENT there lived a nun named Sister Placida. One day she asked Mother Geneviève, who is well known for her skill at drawing: "Mother, for Saint Placid's Day, would you draw me a picture?"

Mother Geneviève did not draw one picture, she drew a hundred and four. It was in this way that *The Life of Little Saint Placid* came to be.

The Life of Little Saint Placid is an exquisite picture treatise on prayer. Tiny as it is, this book is rich in doctrine in the same way as are the windows of French cathedrals. But we of today, with our insatiable greed for illustrated magazines, newspapers, movies, television, are much more remote from spirituality than were our illiterate ancestors of the twelfth and thirteenth centuries; for them sculpture and stained glass held a transparent symbolism. Mother Geneviève has therefore accompanied these drawings with brief texts, as piquant as they are substantial.

A Dominican Father to whom I showed her manuscript exclaimed: "What a find for my sick!" But we people of the world are, all of us, sick; exhausted from wasting time, in a whirl of vain activity, gnawed at by our ego, emotionally overwrought to the breaking-point, ready to die physical death as well as the death of the spirit.

Mother Geneviève's drawings lay a subtle trap for our superficiality. We glance through them, we are charmed by them; the eye is amused, but the spirit, rising from pen strokes to strokes of light, is gradually recollected. It is a divine trick, or better, in Mother Geneviève's words, "a poignant drama in which God and the soul are the players." Our whole heart is "so withdrawn that there is nothing of it left for the world." It was thus that Little Placid was drawn into God.

What miraculous means has Mother Geneviève used to make the workings of prayer visual?

Know, O Placid, that the Interior Life is a life which is INTERIOR...

...the "Yes!" he said to whatever God sent him, both the rain and the sunshine. These are the faces of God, he would say, and raise his head for the kiss.

From one of the pictures we learn how Little Placid prayed:

"Lord, teach me..."
"My son, prayer is spending your life passing into My life."

Another drawing shows us Little Placid's recollection:

> He holds his head erect and his eyes are wide open. Now, how can he be recollected without head cocked and eyes closed? Here is how: in him is the Mystery of God, bottomless well. His whole being is drawn by this Imperious Presence, absorbed little by little, completely engulfed. He is enveloped in God as in a cloak which isolates him from every harmful influence. He goes through life unstained...

Indifferent to his brethren? Not in the least! His love is catching. His sister Flavia takes the veil in the Lady Abbess Saint Scholastica's convent:

> Much surprised, Little Placid spoke of it to Father Master:
> "I didn't say a word about God!"
> "My son, the true apostolate is not what one says but what one is. There is nowadays a kind of loud, busy apostolate. Our apostolate is holiness...We do the little we can to sanctify ourselves and leave the rest to God."

How has a nun, who for nearly forty years has lived behind a convent grille, been able to realize the need for the pictorial element nowadays so exploited in the newsmen's world? Simply because she lives in God and God is up to date. God has no reason to be behind the times in regard to news and the needs of the crowd, to whom he ever shows his loving mercy; eternity includes the present moment.

As did Little Placid, Mother Geneviève lives at a turning-point in history, "in one of those periods in which more than ever it is necessary to hold to the essence of the monastic life rather than to its transitory accidentals." As he did, she embraces "as infallible guides all the present manifestations of the will of God," while Brother Routine would surely die of heart attack at this.

Too bad for Brother Routine, if he holds out for conventional drawing! Mother Geneviève's line has a virile strength and, as need demands, a majestic or a nervous movement; she is not concerned with prettiness. This is the secret of the invincible charm of her picture book. With a few lines she makes the priest bent over the host a massive figure, and the supernatural irradiation of the act of consecration is the more intense in proportion to the monumentality of the one performing it.

God as he is, man as he is and as he becomes through God, in God, while his own life "is swept away by that tremendous torrent of Divine Life." This is what Mother Geneviève shows us, this is what she makes us see with our own eyes.

MARCELLE AUCLAIR

THE LIFE OF LITTLE SAINT PLACID

How Little Placid learned to talk.

Mother pleaded and Nanny scolded,
but all he could say was:
"Yes ...Yes..."

How Little Placid went to the monastery.

When he was two years old, his parents took him to the monastery, although they were a bit uneasy about his speech; to enter the monastery one must be good at languages.

How Saint Benedict received them. He
told them: "Even though in his whole life

he could not say more than 'yes' it would
be enough, sufficit, etiam, bene."

How Little Placid, as soon as he received
the holy habit, clung to God and to his

monastic family, and his heart was so
withdrawn that there was nothing of
it left for the world.

How Nounou didn't understand or accept.

His wet-nurse had a fit
of violent, rebellious grief and her
milk turned. A warning to those who do not
understand nor accept the holy claims of the
Virginity of heart.

How Little Placid begins his day.

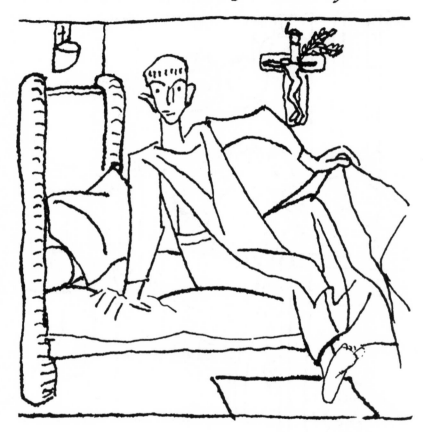

I have risen and have awakened:
I stand up and begin with the dawn.
My Father, who gave me life before
the dawn, I place myself in your presence.

How Little Placid accepts life's
rainy days.

It rains, it rains, shepherdess,
Your sheep's wool will uncurl...
Yes, but Little Placid has nothing
to uncurl, – he's shorn.

How
Little Placid
met trial.

He encounter-
ed the problem
of windows
and doors.
(*Type of the
insoluble*)
Sadly
plagued,
Little Placid
prayed:
"My God,
what is the
solution?"

"My son,
there is
none, and
I would
have none."

(The insoluble continued)

... and that for two reasons: 1. to reveal the category of the fussy; 2. to try the good and make them rise higher. The soul that has made the Sursum Corda is not disturbed over such trifles.

Please, please, for charity's sake, leave the window open.

What Little Placid does when he meets
Father Abbot.

He bows, saying: "Benedicite,"
then adds, very low: "Ave Christe."
The superior is not a comrade here.
No democratic manners!

Little Placid is happy.

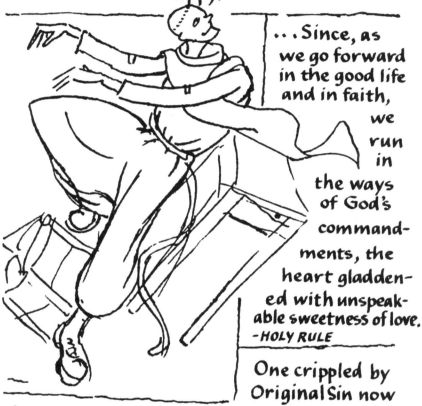

... Since, as we go forward in the good life and in faith, we run in the ways of God's command- ments, the heart gladden- ed with unspeak- able sweetness of love.
—HOLY RULE

One crippled by Original Sin now leaps and dances; the broken pieces are put together again, all that was awry is back in place. Little Placid recovers the integrity of his being. He feels a boundless joy; he pirouettes in his cell. Ambulabam in latitudine. Torrente voluptatis potabis eos.

But his neighbor, Brother Palladius, heard the noise and babbled.

Bowing and scraping, he sputters: "Father, I am obliged...my conscience obliges me... according to the Constitutions... to tell you what my neighbor is up to. For charity's sake, I will not mention his name."

How Little Placid made his profession.

The day dawned on which Little Placid
said: "Promitto in perpetuum." And then,
"Suscipe," then he lay down on the floor for the

Litanies. He fell on the carpet like a rolling ball that at last found its hole. Little Placid was no more, there was only an atom lost in God, ocean of joy. It is done and there is no turning back. The one thing I longed for, I have, & who shall take it from me? The world can tumble down. What does it matter!

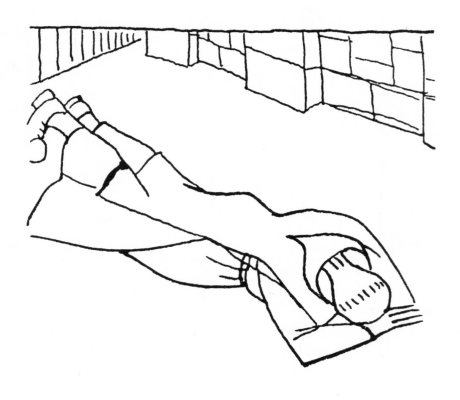

How Little Placid had an extraordinary revelation.

He saw a figure clothed in re- collection. Speaking it said:

"Know, O Placid, that the Interior Life is a life which is Interior." The figure disappeared.

How Little Placid

ran to advise Father Master of the
great revelation that was to turn all
monasteries and all Christendom
upside down. Perhaps we should advise Our Holy Father the Pope?

16

How his aunt, Sister Leocadia, came to see him. Those cats of hers! "What has my baby

coco had to eat? Has he had his little steak, and cream and chee..." "Say, what is this?" "Nephew, yow are naive if you think you can spend your life just loving God! That lacks spice... So, we fill the emptiness of the heart..."

"Begone, Jezabel! To fill with cats and Heaven knows what a heart solemnly consecrated to God! After leaving all the cares of the world supposedly for the one act of loving God then to tear all down for the love of cats! You are a confounded nuisance."

How his little sister Flavia came to see him.
"Hello, Flavette, how are Mama and Papa,

Nanny, kitty?"
And he spent
the whole
day

chatting
with her.

But Flavia
was so taken
by the holi-
ness radiat-
ing from
Little
Placid
that,
afire
with the
conta-
gion of
Divine
Love,
she
took
the
veil
in
the
monastery
of the Lady Abbess Saint Scholastica.

20

Much surprised, Little Placid spoke of it to Father Master. "I didn't say a word about God!" "My son, the true apostolate is not what one says, but what one is. There is nowadays a kind of loud, busy apostolate. Our apostolate is holiness. When a soul rises, it lifts the world up too." We do the little we can to sanctify ourselves and leave the rest to God.

How Little Placid received visitors from the pagan world. "And what do you do all day?"

"Oh, we drink with joy at the fountains of the Saviour." –Amazement– "Yes, to drink and to eat God all day long, that is the monastic life." –Astonishment– "That outdoes your orgies, doesn't it? Here is the kingdom of the Blessed."

Little Placid tries to enumerate the prescriptions of the Ceremonial and cram them into his head. "Not a peaceful moment," he sighs,

"Let's see, do I hold my hands, my feet right? Isn't there someone or something to bow to? And in choir – that's the limit! What a song and dance! Twist, turn, bow – enough to kill you" etc. . . .

Then he becomes Master of Ceremonies and he understands that the ceremonial forms a part of that ascetic system which takes hold of the entire life & that it is the transposition into human terms of the rhythm of life in God. In embracing this vital rhythm one is joined to the Mystical Body of Christ. In choir this ceremonial is an integral part of worship; the Office is not a meditation privatim; it is the Conventual offering, body and soul participating, of the Sacrifice of praise.

How the world and Little Placid see things differently.

The world sees the cloistered walls as a forbidding prison.

Little Placid sees in this prison a sun-filled skylight, open ad astra, letting in the sweet odor of God.

What is the monastic life for
Little Placid?

It is a great
mass of joy
and Little
Placid is in
it over his head, because God is his
food. "O God, it is too much for me
to swallow." "Well then, absorb it, like a
sponge that drinks through all its pores."

Little Placid follows the royal road of Regular Observance. Our Lord leads the way.

The
community
follows,
all in step,
no faster,
no slower,
going to
the same
places,

at the same hour,
every day.
How beautiful it is! You laugh:"Not so
hard.""Well, my friend, come and try it."

How Father Saint Benedict and Little Placid loved each other.

"O my blessed Father! Noblest cedar in the gardens of the Church, filled with the spirit of all the Just!"

"O Placid, little jewel from paradise! Little ray of light falling from Eden into my hands! Just like you are my true sons."

From his cell Little Placid looks at the abbatial buildings, surrounded by the cloister, joined together by the church as the circle of a ring is closed by its precious stone. These walls tell the manner of life led within them. They are the mould in which are formed the lives that flow there. Lives in the grip of a discipline which from every side directs them toward the Church. Unity of life.

The Abbey is a world, an entity. Its centre is in its very midst. The man in the street may have said this & yet it is a little-known fact. God does not give himself to those who do not love; they are then seized by a centrifugal force which propels them beyond the enclosure — only their feet remain inside. Like tops they spin round and round, seeking in creatures what they will not seek in God, bogging down in their own mire, madly in love with themselves. But Little Placid knows, as do many others, that in the heart of the Abbey there is a life-giving spring.

What is this well, if not the sacrament of this hidden thing? Encircled by its necklace of graceful arches, it whispers: Si quis sitit veniat ad me et bibat. Little Placid knew how to draw water — by loving observance of the Rule,

through the liturgy, prayer, listening for God's secret whisperings, by the "Yes" he said to whatever God sent him, both the rain & the sunshine. These are the faces of God, he would say, and raise his head to receive the kiss. In this way he entered

a forest of undreamed delights, of re-
freshment, of bewitching perfumes.
Under its spell, he buried his virgin
heart in the virgin heart of the Abbey
forever.

And there he was, poor little nothing-
at-all Placid — and by what right?
Overwhelmed with joy, his heart
poured out in gratitude, he wept.

How Little Placid prayed.

"Lord, teach me . . ."
"My son, prayer is spending your
life passing into My Life."

Little Placid's prayer.
(From Saint Gregory of Nazianzen)

How many joys for me in each of the Mysteries of Christ! The conse-quence of them all is my perfection, my restoration, my return to the innocence of the first Adam.

He makes me God. How much rejoicing for me in all the events of His Life; what mystery in my inner life!

What the Office means for Little Placid.

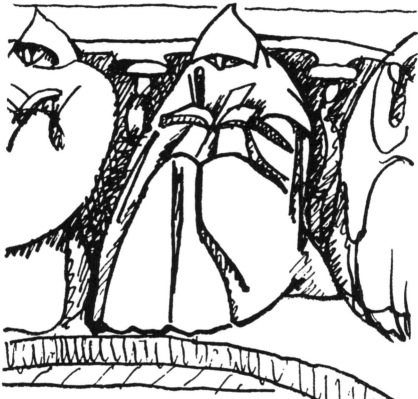

"To sing one's life and live one's song."
What is this song and what is this life
which it opens up for us? To whom do we speak
in such terms? What is our relationship

to Him?
Little Placid
found himself
placed object-
ively before
God.
The Liturgy
put into his
mouth words he
never dared utter.
His words formed
his thought and
his thought formed
his being.
And so, the Litur-
gy enfolded him
as in a mould, and
when it had trans-
formed him, then rose
to God as the ex-
pression of his own
being, Little Placid.

38

Little Placid

immerses himself in the Divine Mysteries;
he wears them like a cope which covers his
humanity infirma et sauciata. And the
Angels wait on him, seeing in him the
Image of the Son of God.

What recollection means to Little Placid.

He holds his head erect and his eyes wide open. But how can he be recollected without head cocked and eyes closed? Here is how: in him is the Mystery of God. Bottomless well. His whole being is drawn by this Imperious Presence, absorbed little by little, completely engulfed. He is enveloped in God as in a cloak which isolates him from every harmful influence. He goes through life, unstained . . .

What is the Mass
for Little Placid?

It is the summing up of his whole being,
all his strength added to the Humanity
of Our Lord offered to God; the one
act in life "et nunc et semper."

The Mass is over.

How can that act be finished which constitutes all life and is eternal? Little Placid reflects: "God, in coming to us, subjected Himself to our condition of life, to the law of time, to the multiplicity of our

nature and to the liberty of our will. The
offering of the Lamb who taketh away the sins
of the world lasts an hour of Time. The Redemp-
tion is communicated to us provided that we
say an incessant "yes". Another kind of Mass
begins now. The cowl is taken off.

There are two
powers in the will:
the concupiscible appetite which desires
the good, and the irascible appetite which
fights to possess the good. Good servants,
bad masters. On the loose since Original
Sin, they go dashing after their desires.
Here is the source of all wars – foreign,
civil, domestic, and the revolt of

the flesh against the spirit and all the abomi—
nations that we see around us. Monastic discipline tends to restore order in those who
submit to it. Little Placid submitted unre-
servedly and won the victory over himself.
A sight fairer than all the heavens! He had
bridled the two appetites and harness-
ed them to the chariot of his spiritual
life: the one desiring God, the
other fighting to possess God.

Little Placid releases his COMBATIVE & ABSOLUTE energies:

"Go out to meet the thousand manifestations of God's will; embrace them well and lose yourselves in them. If the flesh and the devil get in your way, run them through." That is what it means to accomplish and perfect consecration and belonging to the Sovereign God. That is the meaning of penance: love shedding all that holds it back. So, don't let anyone tell us that we lead a life of penance to expiate the sins of the world and to avoid wars or for this or for that. We lead a life of love by means of penance for no other reason than love, which is its own justification.

Little Placid gives orders to Combative and to Absolute: "In the conquest of the Promised Land, which is intimacy with God, take care to exterminate the neighboring tribes—Jebusites and Hittites. No quarter! Ut nullum praeter Eum Amatorem admittam."

Seeing that the battle was waxing hot, Little Placid released   EXCESSIVE :

" Go and act according to the dynamism God has given you, and do
not listen to the partisans of the
middle way."

"And remember, to hit the bull's eye, you must aim higher."

A manifestation of the Will of God: WORK.
1. Obedience to the commandment: Thou shalt

earn thy
bread with the sweat of thy brow.
2. Necessity: He who does not work will
not eat. 3. Work channels disordered
energies into the way of obedience; it con-
tinually frees the monk from self-slavery; it
serves as an outlet for the overflow of dynamism,

for interior angers. It is the commonest
expression of obedience, the easiest way
to ex-
change
our
will

for the   Divine Life. It is an
expansion   of the other two forms
of work: the Opus Dei and inter—
ior asceticism. If one of these three
kinds of work is missing, lack of balance
is inevitable.

But does Little Placid only work at what the books call "mean and lowly jobs?"

What does it matter? Had he built cathedrals, does that make the man? Even the most sublime human activity is as nothing beside the Divine Activity of God's life in us. That makes the man.

How Little Placid asks a permission of Father Abbot.

"Dear Father, may I please hang a plumb-line from the ceiling of our cell?"

"Why, my son?" "To have always before my eyes the image of the straight line which must be the armature of my soul, and the road from my soul to God.

And this vertical line tends to veer to one side and to wind like a corkscrew." "Why, yes, dear son, you may, and I will come and help you."

—" Put also some figures suggesting the Absolute: the right angle, the circle. There is ONE right angle – integrity. There are thousands of oblique angles, and they are mediocrity. O my son,

respect in your-
self the Absolute.
Two powers
work for our
destruction:
1. Vile Mediocrity,
which
tears down
all the

dignity of
our being;
be hard as
steel in
resisting it.

2. The HOLY CROSS, which de-
stroys all our short-
comings. Give yourself
to it with total and
loving surrender."

DOMINE, DA MIHI SCIRE QUOD SCIENDUM EST

Little Placid was at his studies.
The catechism says: There are four wounds
resulting from Original Sin: ignorance,
concupiscence, malice and weakness. It is
just as unlawful to abandon oneself to ignorance as it is to the other three. Ignorance
has replaced infused knowledge: the understanding is *tabula rasa* and is no more.

Religious ignorance leads the merry dance of her light-headed children.

Directed to God, the understanding informs the will. Our activities are measured by the extent of our understanding. The *tabula rasa* must be strengthened with doctrine.

Little Placid studies Theology.

The science of sciences that one never learns because it is infinite and because the intelligence and the will hold back. Little Placid threw himself into this course and drew from it the light for his eyes and warmth for his heart.

Little Placid learned the dogma of Original Sin.

Ecce, ego sum

He was so struck by it that he made a funny but expressive drawing to illustrate for himself the frightful nakedness of man stripped of God. He especially aimed at ignorance and weakness. If Christians and even monks and nuns believed this dogma, would they be so full of themselves as is often the case?

How the Monastery moved and what Little Placid did. Will he

hold out for his schedule of the past ten years? "My prayer, my reading, and then move all you want." Not at all. His supple intelligence has understood that one must obey with understanding.

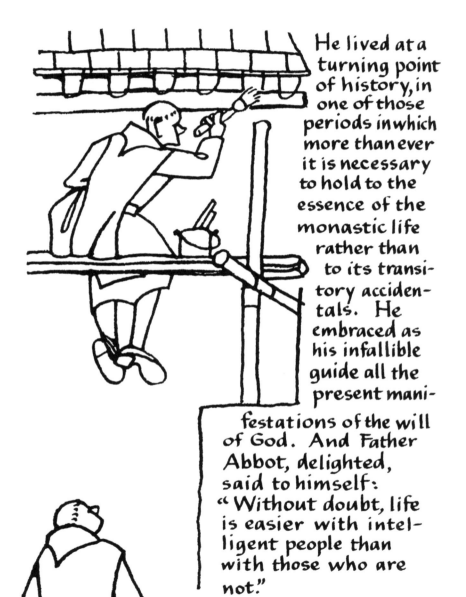

He lived at a turning point of history, in one of those periods in which more than ever it is necessary to hold to the essence of the monastic life rather than to its transitory accidentals. He embraced as his infallible guide all the present manifestations of the will of God. And Father Abbot, delighted, said to himself: "Without doubt, life is easier with intelligent people than with those who are not."

SIMPLE QUESTION.

".. But, my dear Father, the lesson of the war was wasted! The world was not converted! etc. etc. . . ." Little Placid reflected: And the good Fathers, have they been converted? And what about me? This Me which is the only mission land over which I have any control & of which I must give account.

How, through imprudence, Little Placid committed murder.

All he said was: "The vows & the Rule are made to be observed & the Office to be lived." Hearing this, Father Routine suffered a heart attack & died on the spot.

Christus natus est nobis, venite adoremus.

Little Placid, at dawn of Christmas day, goes to see the created Face of the Creator. He took a book by a great contemplative and read: "There is no reality outside the vision of this eternally blessed Face."

... in illius inveniamur
forma in quo tecum est nostra
substantia. And what is this Form?
Reversal of values. Complete distrust of
human activity, of everything human.
That is the contemplative life.

Further on he read: "The strong man is he who is firmly rooted in the weakness of Christ." The fall of that fictitious strength of the egotist, of the ridiculous frenzy of the ant who thinks it can build the world. Reduced to nothing, he said: "Lord, I can do no more."

"Sufficit tibi, Placid, gratia mea."

And as his human strength left him, God's strength filled him.

How Little Placid celebrated the anniversary of his profession: Trembling with fear and joy, he takes his place at the

wedding banquet of Christ the King, his bridegroom. He dizzily measures the abyss of grace in which he is submerged and the abyss of misery from which he has escaped. O Jesus, Mary, if you had not said for me that word: Promitto, how could I have said it? And because of that little word,

which is yours more than mine, Lord, you
lead me into an en-
chanted world, into
the undreamed-of
sweetness of intimacy.
O gaudium! O Lae-
titia! Posuisti super
me manum tuam.

Little Placid shrinks to the tininess of a
minnow. And that is humility: one's
own life swept away by that tremendous
torrent of Divine Life.

One Pente-
cost afternoon
voices were
heard in Little
Placid's cell.
Father Prior is
notified:"What!
Conversation
in a cell?"
He enters
and sees Little
Placid, all
radiant, com-
pletely surround-
ed by the splen-
dor de flamine
sacro. The
Seven Gifts were there, the seven energies
of Divine Love, and they were speaking:
Counsel, Knowledge, Understanding, Wisdom
were repeating the words of the Divine Office
and extracting for him their hidden sweet—
ness: something like those candies one
sucks a bit and which suddenly open and
yield their delicious liquid. Piety had
nothing to say

because holy tears were already streaming down Little Placid's cheeks. *Fear* spoke: "If you but knew the gift of God which you bear in a fragile vessel! Fear to lose it, as you fear hell itself." *Fortitude* spoke:

"Let go your feeble strength – I am your strength. All the Gifts are ordered to an heroic life: we carry aloft, beyond anything human

the one we
possess."

Little
Placid
felt a thrill
something

like falling
from a fifth-story
window. But
an Element,
a Power
intervened.
"Have no fear,
you fall in God."
O Peace! O
Sessio! O laeta
quies of one
who falls into
God!
"Lord, I have
used up the
Admirabile
Commercium –
what is left
for me on
earth?"

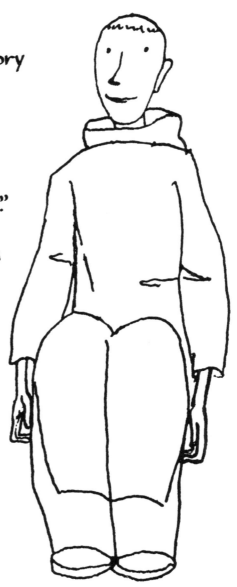

He put the Sevenfold Spirit, the Donum Dei Altissimi, into a bag. "The only thing I can call MINE." The bag is invisible to the eyes of the flesh & Little Placid guards it day & night. He took Understanding out of the bag & went to behold the Corpus Christi.

There is more here than the Victim of the Sacrifice, the abiding of our Lord. All the mysteries of his life, in mysterio, in Sacramento, socius.

He offers himself ad contem-
plandum et ad imitandum.
We cannot offer this God-
victim without participating
in His
Divinity
through His
Humanity.
Because
this inter-
course with
Him is a
divine cap-
acity which
nothing, not
even hell,
can take
from us.

77

When a sacrifice is offered, the Victim is eaten.
But this Victim is God!
Abyss! He seizes us,
absorbs us, assimilates
us to Himself.

And yet I am not an-
nihilated: I am still Me,
Little Placid, fattened
and satisfied and

hearty, after this nourishment and in
possession of my free will to make use of
God as I wish. "My God,
is it only for a day?"
"I cut eternity into small
pieces called 'days'
adapted to your
little possibilities,
little men. I cut
my own Self
into small
hosts in order
to give you
one each day.
I cut continu-
ity into dis-
continuity to
multiply the
ineffable act
that gives Me

to you &
makes you
repeat the
'Yes' that
gives you
to Me.
And what
is the an-
swer I get from un-
grateful souls? 'To make
your bed in the morning, to get
into it at night...I'm sick of it..'

Gift of Knowledge, where are you?
Explain to those sleepy heads that
hidden under this shower of prosaic
little chores that falls on them every day,
is my FACE, veiled and bending down
to kiss them. But they cower and
open their
umbrellas."

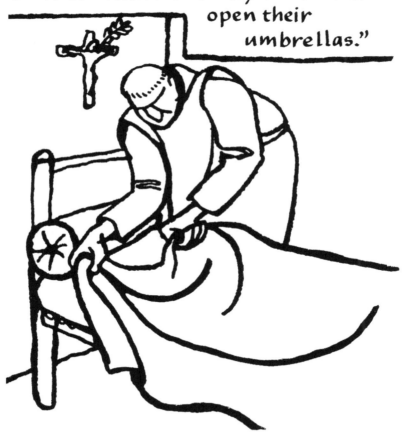

Little Placid whirled from abyss to abyss. With rigorous logic, link was welded to link, and he could not see the end of the chain. He then put Intelligence back and took out Wisdom. A new world of knowl-

edge! He could now savor the notions provided by Intelligence. He let himself dissolve in God and by this act of love, captured Him completely.

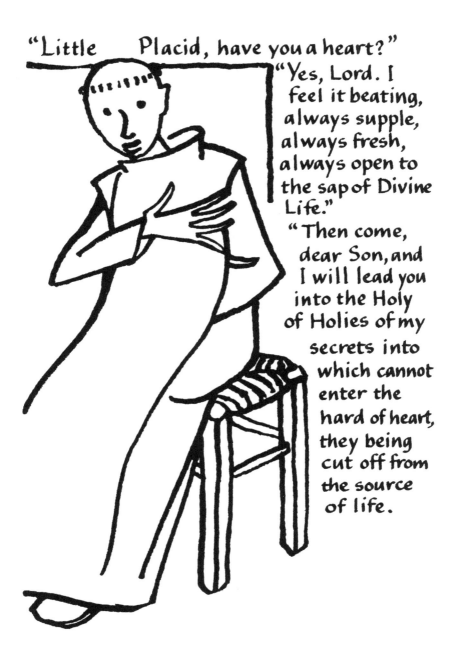

"Little Placid, have you a heart?"

"Yes, Lord. I feel it beating, always supple, always fresh, always open to the sap of Divine Life."

"Then come, dear Son, and I will lead you into the Holy of Holies of my secrets into which cannot enter the hard of heart, they being cut off from the source of life.

MY DIVINE
HEART,
which is my
life and the
life of all that
lives.

Outside
this Love which
thrusts ME into
MYSELF and into ME
my creatures made
in my IMAGE, outside
this Love is only
DEATH."

Little Placid is absorbed by the mystery of life. Accedit ad cor altum. In the silence of this abyss he feels the incessant soaring of his heart in flight to its Source and End. No retreat in self. The I falls dead. Here at last is life. Who can tell the power of this Vital Act, its Peace & its Happiness!

85

How Little Placid met temptation.

The Devil, seeing this exquisite flower God was keeping for Himself in His closed garden, resolved to pluck it & throw it outside to wither & die.

He brought his same old arsenal: "Go back to your dear parents who are weeping over your absence. Why annihilate yourself in this incomplete life? Do you even have a vocation? And to what? Prayer? The search for God? Impossible illusions. Our time is meant for action. Act on your own; don't count on God. So many souls are calling you."

He opened his ear to the Devil's intoxicating venom.

And the cross
weighed more
heavily on Jesus'
shoulders.

Completely over-
come he started
to take off
the "habitum
sanctae con-
versationis"
to trample
under foot
his Supreme
Dignity, his
one Happi-
ness and
the fruit
of the
Lord's
Passion.

But those who loved
him cried out in his
behalf to the Mother of
Mercy, Memorare. . . .

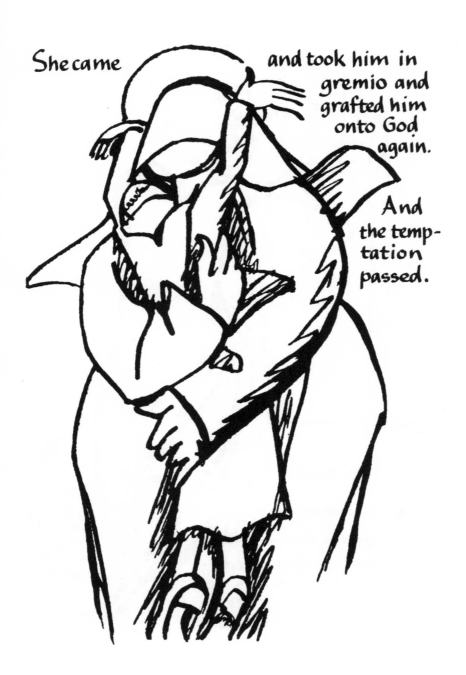

She came and took him in gremio and grafted him onto God again.

And the temptation passed.

His heart fluttering he sat down in the cloisters. O God! Torrente voluptatis potabis eos. The prodigal son has recovered more than he lost. Little Placid let himself sink in this joy.

He laughed a sweet little laugh of love, this little nothing-at-all Placid over whom God's desire hovers.

Satan came to see the results of his diplomacy; but Little Placid was armed. "Why do you seek me, did you not know that I must be about my Father's business?"

Little Placid has just
overcome the shoals

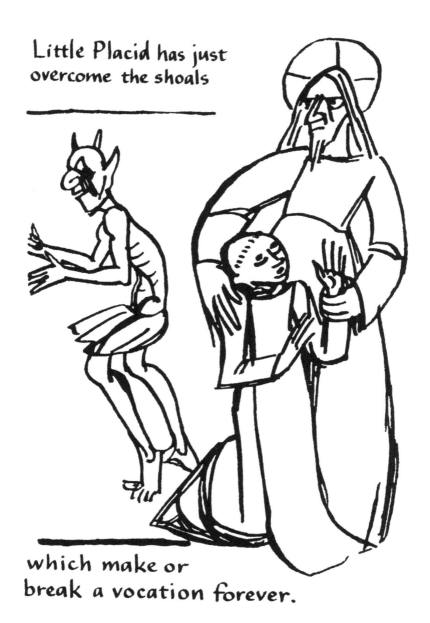

which make or
break a vocation forever.

How Little Placid went to an exhibition of abstract art.

"Since you lead an exclusively religious life, you must understand these things? – Obviously it is the highest Art, which frees line from the limitations of the concrete in order to turn it into the vehicle of thought."

" But that presupposes that there is a Thought & that the symbol that expresses it is accessible to all."

" Not at all: You do violence to pure art by wishing to make it express something. It is all rhythm of lines, of colors, masses. It comes from Superman and is addressed to Superman."

"That's possible, dear friend. But, if so, I must withdraw because I am only a Man, with both feet on the ground and I don't understand pure abstraction. When God, who is Master of the arts and Father of common sense, wished to show us something of the ineffable abstract, He began by clothing the concrete - this was the Incarnation. It is in this way that He tells us the most sublime truths. It is the norm of all our human efforts."
" Nevertheless, you cannot deny the value of line in itself?"
' Surely not, & you are entirely free to go no further;

as for myself, I should like to say something. There is an enormous Mystery in me which envelops me completely, a life, an essence of life, from which I drink my fullness: a surging wave overthrowing with the force of a tank all ready-made theories; it would express itself, find a voice; it attains form through the very vitality of its well-spring. That is my Art."

How Little
Placid knew
illness.

Suppression of normal activity. A turning point in his spiritual life; a new view of the world. Energy is no longer used to exercise the powers of Being but to accept the destruction of Being wrought by suffering.

Inactive, wasted, as short-sight-
ed folk would say. But he felt
welling up inside him the revelation of a new
life. Until today his spiritual life was so much
smoke, far-seeing attempts, sparring exercises in
view of the real fight. Now is the hour. He has
reached the heart of the citadel; it is hand-to-hand
combat with God. Freed of health, human
activity, the natural joy of living (just so
many illusions which cause one to shuffle
about within the same narrow circle) he
clings purely and simply to the Divine Action.
It is a pure act stripped of contingent
modalities.

What Little Placid said to Father Infirmarian:

When you see that I am dying, call the Precentor to intone the Exsultet jam Angelica . . . O quam glorifica . . . and the little Alleluias of the Easter Vigil, sweet murmur of ecstasy, silver bells of Paradise announcing the eternal dawn. Ecce adsum.

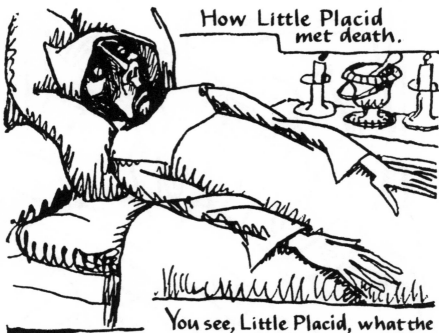

How Little Placid met death.

You see, Little Placid, what the Mass is? The full return to the Father. You suffered at Mass and Communion, feeling you were still yourself before God and not absorbed in Him. Death was lacking. Now the obstacle is laid low - you are face to face with Him. The fall of the first man is atoned for in you. The goal, success, consummation, fullness of the harvest crowning the sowing. Death gives fecundity to your whole life. Blessed Little Placid, whose whole life has been a Mass; and the Mass all his Life.

Promitto stabilitatem conversionem morum meorum et obedientiam secundum Regulam Sancti Patris Benedicti.

IN
PARA-
DI-
SUM
DEDU-
CANT
TE

ANGE-
LI